Contents

Assessm[ent]
The Gre[at...]
page 2

Written by
Alison Hawes

Illustrated by
Alan Marks

Series editor **Dee Reid**

Before reading
The Green Cloud

Characters

Tommy    Eric    Fred    Jack

Tricky words

ch1 p3	periscope	ch2 p11	bellowed
ch1 p6	gazing	ch3 p13	gasped
ch1 p6	stared	ch3 p15	signalled
ch2 p9	immediately	ch4 p19	nervously

Story starter

In the First World War Tommy and Eric lied about their ages and joined the army. The boys were in a British trench fighting the Germans. One day, Tommy was on sentry duty. He was using his periscope to watch the enemy trench across No Man's Land.

The Green Cloud

Chapter One

Tommy was finding it really hard to keep awake. He closed his eyes, then quickly opened them again. *I must stay awake*, he thought as he looked through his periscope at the enemy trench opposite. For once, nothing was happening.

Tommy turned round to look at the people near him in the trench. His friends, Eric and Fred, were reading quietly. To their left, a young soldier called Jack lay asleep by a pile of sandbags.

Tommy was pleased to see no one was looking his way. *It won't hurt if I just lean on the trench wall and close my eyes for a minute*, he thought. Moments later, he was asleep.

Fred stopped reading and called out to Tommy. "Anything happening?" he asked. Tommy snapped his eyes open and looked at his watch. He had been asleep for ages! He quickly began looking through his periscope again.

"No, it's still quiet," he said.

"It's *too* quiet," said Fred. "I think the enemy are up to something!"

Tommy carried on gazing at the enemy trenches. There was no sign of anything moving. Then he saw something he had never seen before. He stared at it for a moment, wondering what it could be. Then he called out to Fred.

"I think you should come and look at this," Tommy called.
"Why? What is it?" asked Fred.
"I'm not sure," Tommy answered, "but I don't like the look of it!"

Chapter Two

Tommy stepped aside and let Fred look through the periscope. Fred could see a thick green cloud rolling along the ground. The wind was blowing the cloud straight at the British trench.

Fred knew immediately what it was.
He groaned and his face went as white
as a sheet.

"Quick, Tommy! Sound the alarm. It's gas
– *poison* gas!" he roared, as he pulled his
gas mask over his head.

Tommy jumped up onto the fire step that
ran along the wall of the trench and
sounded the alarm.

"Gas attack!" he yelled, before he pulled
his own mask on.

All along the trench, everyone dropped what they were doing, put on their gas masks and climbed up onto the step with Tommy. Everyone, that is, apart from Jack. When the alarm woke him, it had taken him a few seconds to understand what was happening.

Tommy looked through the little windows in his mask. Jack still didn't have his gas mask on.

"Get your mask on!" Tommy yelled through his gas mask. "The gas is almost here!" Jack was afraid. His hands were shaking so much, he couldn't even get his mask out of his bag. Then, as the green gas rolled over the top of the trench, he suddenly went pale, stopped trying to get his mask on and ran off down the trench.

"Stop!" bellowed Fred.

Chapter Three

Fred jumped down into the trench and grabbed Jack as he sprinted past. "Don't be frightened, lad," Fred said, as he helped Jack pull on his mask. "You'll be safe up on the step with the rest of us." Jack was scared and trembling all over but he followed Fred up onto the step.

As the trench filled up with the deadly gas, Fred found himself fighting for breath. He turned towards Eric.

"Help me!" he gasped.

"Something is wrong with Fred!" Eric shouted at Tommy.

Tommy spotted a small split in the side of Fred's mask.

"Quick!" Tommy yelled at Eric. "Get another mask out of Fred's bag. This mask has a hole in it and the gas is getting in."
Eric did as he was told.
"I'm going to count to three," Tommy shouted to Fred, "and then I'm going to take off your mask."

Fred nodded that he understood. He held his breath as Tommy tore off the split mask and Eric pulled another mask over Fred's head.

"Are you alright now?" asked Tommy. Fred leaned on the trench wall, taking in breath after breath. He pointed at his chest and throat and shook his head, but then he signalled to let them know that he was OK.

Tommy picked up the periscope and looked through it.

"Oh no!" he cried.

"What's wrong now?" asked Eric.

"It's hard to see through the cloud of gas," Tommy replied, "but I think the enemy soldiers are coming our way."

Chapter Four

Tommy put down the periscope and carefully looked over the muddy top of the trench. It was a dangerous thing to do but he could see things more clearly without the periscope.

He could just make out a group of enemy soldiers climbing out of their trench.

"Well?" said Eric.

"I was right," Tommy said. "They're coming for us!"

Tommy watched as the enemy soldiers slowly picked their way through the rocks and barbed wire in front of their trench. Then he watched them march into No Man's Land.

"They will soon be here," Tommy said. "They have reached No Man's Land."

Jack was frightened and started to tremble. He tried to pull off his gas mask. "We're all going to be killed! I don't want to die!" he screamed.

Fred grabbed Jack and spoke quietly into his ear. "Sssh! You're not going to die. If we stick together, we'll be alright, but I need you to stop that noise. Do you understand?"

Jack fell silent and, all along the step, the British soldiers waited nervously for the attack to start.

Then, just as the enemy soldiers got half way across No Man's Land, something happened.

"Look!" Tommy whispered, pointing at the gas cloud.

The gas cloud was no longer coming towards them. The wind was now sending it the other way! The enemy soldiers were not able to see where they were going. They turned around and dashed back to their own trench.

Tommy and his friends couldn't believe their luck! Everyone around them gave a loud cheer.
"Didn't I tell you everything would be alright?" grinned Fred.

Quiz

Text detective

- **p4** Why is Tommy pleased that no one is looking his way?
- **p4** Why does Tommy pretend that it doesn't matter if he just closes his eyes?
- **p5** How can you tell that Fred is an experienced soldier?
- **p9** Why do you think Tommy warned the other soldiers before putting on his own gas mask?
- **p11** What word describes how Jack feels about the poison gas?
- **p12** What evidence is there that Fred is a good leader?
- **p15** Why do you think Fred pointed at his chest and throat and shook his head?
- **p17** Why do you think the enemy decided to attack when they did?
- **p20** Do you feel sorry for the enemy soldiers?
- **p21** How do you think Tommy and Eric felt at the end?

What do you think?

Why was poison gas used in the World War I? Do you think it was right to use it as a weapon? Was it any worse than bullets and bombs?

Quiz

Word detective

- **p5** Which verb shows that Tommy wakes up quickly?
- **p5** Why is the word 'too' in italics?
- **p9** Find a simile. Why is it effective?
- **p11** Which speech verb shows that Fred is determined to stop Jack?
- **p13** Why is the word 'gasped' a good choice of speech verb?
- **p19** What two words are contracted in 'we'll'?
- **p19** Which adverb shows how the British soldiers are feeling?
- **p20** Find a compound sentence joined by 'and'.

Vocabulary

- **p3** Find a word meaning 'on the other side'.
- **p5** Find a word meaning 'a long time'.
- **p6** Find a word meaning 'looking steadily'.
- **p11** Find a word meaning 'trembling'.
- **p20** Find a word meaning 'hurried'.

HA! HA!

Q: What kind of tea stops you feeling scared?

A: Safe-ty!

Published by Pearson Education Limited, a company incorporated in England and Wales, having its registered office at Edinburgh Gate, Harlow, Essex CM20 2JE.
Registered company number: 872828

www.pearsonschools.co.uk

Pearson is a registered trademark of Pearson plc

Text © Pearson Education Limited 2013

The right of Alison Hawes to be identified as the author of this work has been asserted by her in accordance with the Copyright, Designs and Patents Act 1988.

First published 2013

22
10

British Library Cataloguing in Publication Data is available from the British Library on request.

ISBN: 978 0 435 15257 4

Copyright notice
All rights reserved. No part of this publication may be reproduced in any form or by any means (including photocopying or storing it in any medium by electronic means and whether or not transiently or incidentally to some other use of this publication) without the written permission of the copyright owner, except in accordance with the provisions of the Copyright, Designs and Patents Act 1988 or under the terms of a licence issued by the Copyright Licensing agency, Saffron House, 6-10 Kirby Street, London ECIN 8TS (www.cla.co.uk). Applications for the copyright owner's written permission should be addressed to the publisher.

Designed by Bigtop
Original illustrations © Pearson Education Limited 2013
Illustrated by Alan Marks
Printed and bound in Great Britain
Font © Pearson Education Ltd
Teaching notes by Dee Reid

Acknowledgements
We would like to thank the following schools for their invaluable help in the development and trialling of this course:

Callicroft Primary School, Bristol; Castlehill Primary School, Fife; Elmlea Junior School, Bristol; Lancaster School, Essex; Llanidloes School, Powys; Moulton School, Newmarket; Platt C of E Primary School, Kent; Sherborne Abbey CE VC Primary School, Dorset; Upton Junior School, Poole; Whitmore Park School, Coventry.